I hope you enjoy this book.
Please make sure to visit:

https://pambrossman.com/pbjournals

To see the other notebooks, journals, planners and adult coloring books in the **Evolving HQ series.**

COPYRIGHT © PAMBROSSMAN.COM - ALL RIGHTS RESERVED WORLDWIDE.
THIS PRODUCT IS PROTECTED UNDER INTERNATIONAL AND NATIONAL
COPYRIGHT LAWS 2020

good vibes

Let your light shine

You

ARE THE ANSWER

believe

Draw or describe what your dream life looks like

SLOW AND STEADY

live
your
dream.

Unstoppable!

Appreciate | Attract | Achieve

Share Below

3 things you are grateful for today

1 thing you want to attract today

1 thing you want to achieve today!

3 things I'm grateful for today:

1.
2.
3.

1 thing I would love to attract into my day today:

1 thing I want to achieve today:

hope

What a great year!

Believe

IN YOUR DREAMS

One day at a time

What was awesome about your day today?

hello Sunshine

inspire

Limitless!

Appreciate | Attract | Achieve

Share Below

3 things you are grateful for today

1 thing you want to attract today

1 thing you want to achieve today!

3 things I'm grateful for today:

1.
2.
3.

1 thing I would love to attract into my day today:

1 thing I want to achieve today:

reach for the stars!

Chill

Beautiful

INSIDE & OUT

Better Days Ahead

What do you want to achieve by the end of the year?

chill out

Grateful

Confident!

Appreciate | Attract | Achieve

Share Below

3 things you are grateful for today

1 thing you want to attract today

1 thing you want to achieve today!

3 things I'm grateful for today:

1.
2.
3.

1 thing I would love to attract into my day today:

1 thing I want to achieve today:

have a nice day

Happy

Born
TO ACHIEVE & SUCCEED!

stay groovy

What's on your dream bucket list for this year?

It's All Good

life is good

Successful!

Appreciate | Attract | Achieve

Share Below

3 things you are grateful for today

1 thing you want to attract today

1 thing you want to achieve today!

3 things I'm grateful for today:

1.
2.
3.

1 thing I would love to attract into my day today:

1 thing I want to achieve today:

YOU CAN DO IT!

BE FABULOUS

Driven

& PASSIONATE!

DO YOUR Thing

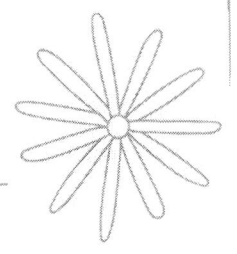

3 things you're grateful for today?

1.

2.

3.

Think it Want it Get it

You're AMAZING

Thoughtful!

Appreciate | Attract | Achieve

Share Below

3 things you are grateful for today

1 thing you want to attract today

1 thing you want to achieve today!

3 things I'm grateful for today:

1.
2.
3.

1 thing I would love to attract into my day today:

1 thing I want to achieve today:

DON'T LOSE FOCUS

POSITIVE
VIBES

Success

WAS NEVER IN QUESTION!

1.

2.

Name 4 things you're awesome at?

3.

4.

Bee Yourself

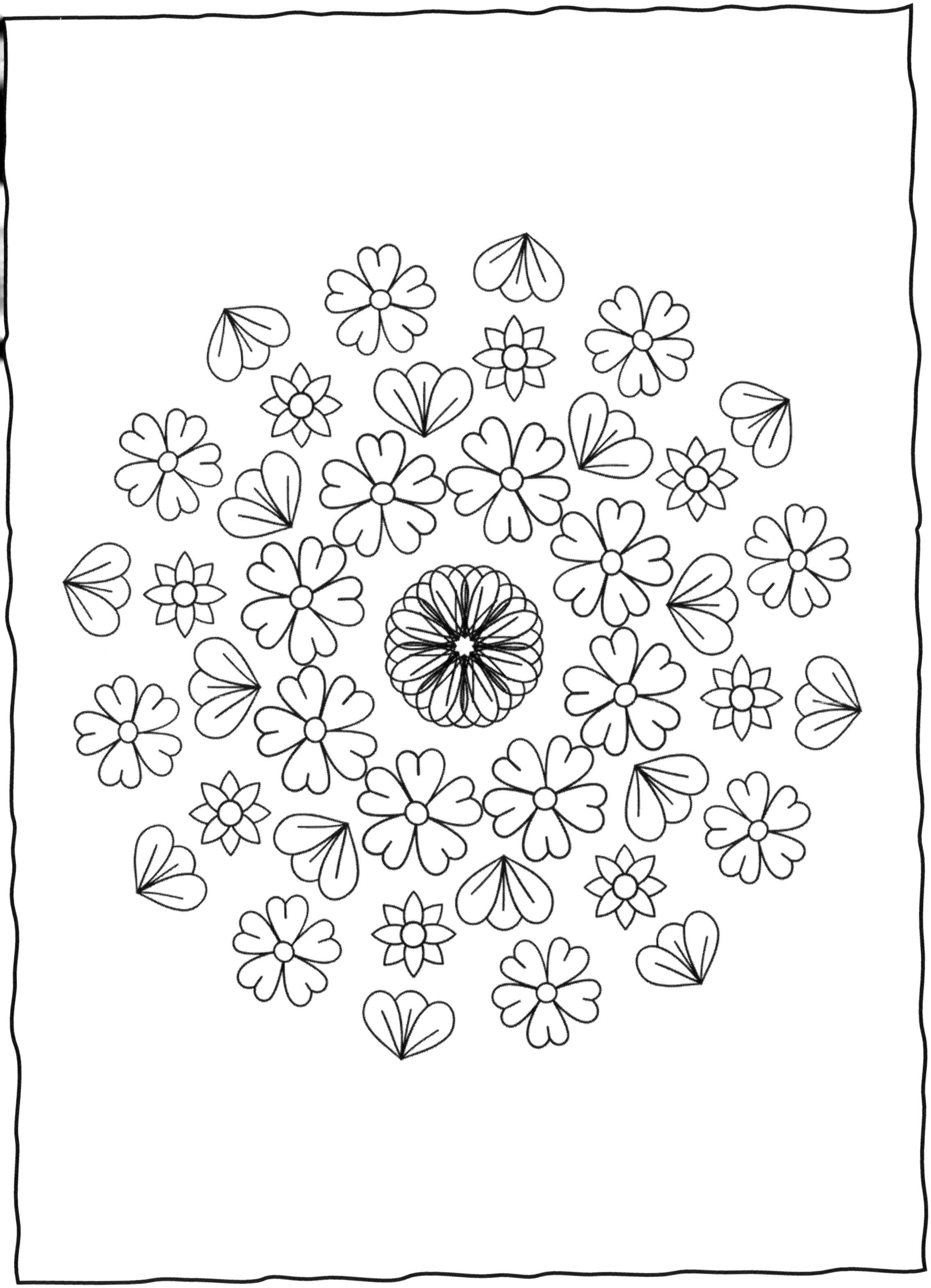

Generous!

Appreciate | Attract | Achieve

Share Below

3 things you are grateful for today

1 thing you want to attract today

1 thing you want to achieve today!

3 things I'm grateful for today:

1.
2.
3.

1 thing I would love to attract into my day today:

1 thing I want to achieve today:

live laugh love

Write 20 positive words to describe you!

Joy

I know

I CAN, SO I WILL!

enjoy every moment.

5 things you love about yourself:

1.

2.

3.

4.

5.

dream

Dream big

Kind!

Appreciate | Attract | Achieve

Share Below

3 things you are grateful for today

1 thing you want to attract today

1 thing you want to achieve today!

3 things I'm grateful for today:

1.
2.
3.

1 thing I would love to attract into my day today.

1 thing I want to achieve today:

DREAM BIG, WORK HARD, MAKE IT *happen.*

Spiky
on the outside

Sweet
on the inside

Say Yes

TO YOU!

POSITIVITEA

Someone read your tea leaves and said you have lots of good fortune coming. What do you want it to be?

YES you can!

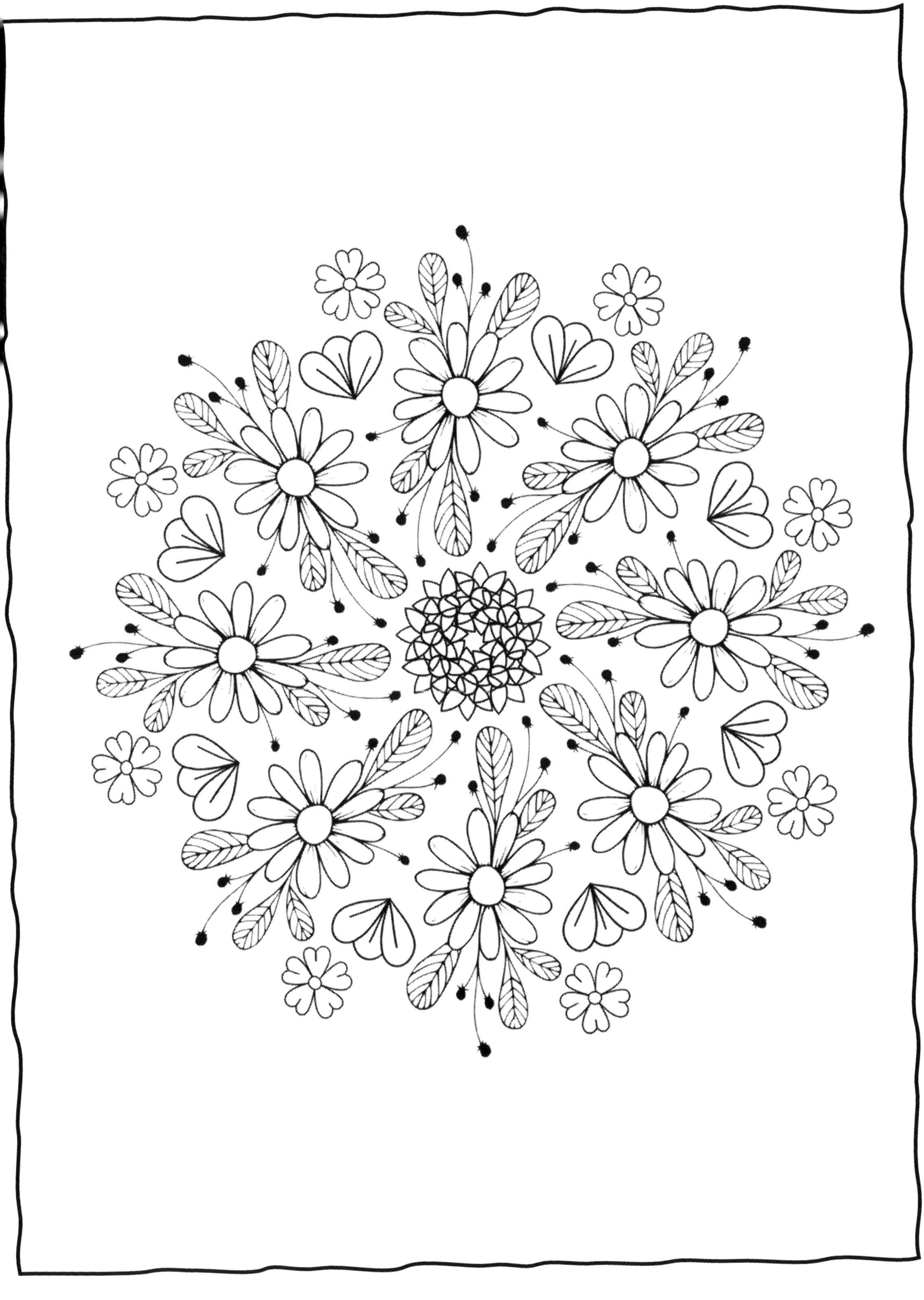

Genius!

Appreciate | Attract | Achieve

Share Below

3 things you are grateful for today

1 thing you want to attract today

1 thing you want to achieve today!

3 things I'm grateful for today:

1.
2.
3.

1 thing I would love to attract into my day today:

1 thing I want to achieve today:

take care of your mind

Keep going

Stretch

YOU'RE WORTH IT!

do it for you

List 3 positive new habits you're going to start this year:

1.

2.

3.

Just Bee Awesome

BELIEVE IN YOURSELF

Beautiful

Prosperous!

Appreciate | Attract | Achieve

Share Below

3 things you are grateful for today

1 thing you want to attract today

1 thing you want to achieve today!

3 things I'm grateful for today:

1.
2.
3.

1 thing I would love to attract into my day today:

1 thing I want to achieve today:

yaas

love

Focus

ON YOUR VISION DAILY!

You can!

This year's top 5 goals

1.

2.

3.

4.

5.

Fearless

be yourself

Funny!

Appreciate | Attract | Achieve

Share Below

3 things you are grateful for today

1 thing you want to attract today

1 thing you want to achieve today!

3 things I'm grateful for today:

1.
2.
3.

1 thing I would love to attract into my day today:

1 thing I want to achieve today:

Believe, Build, Become

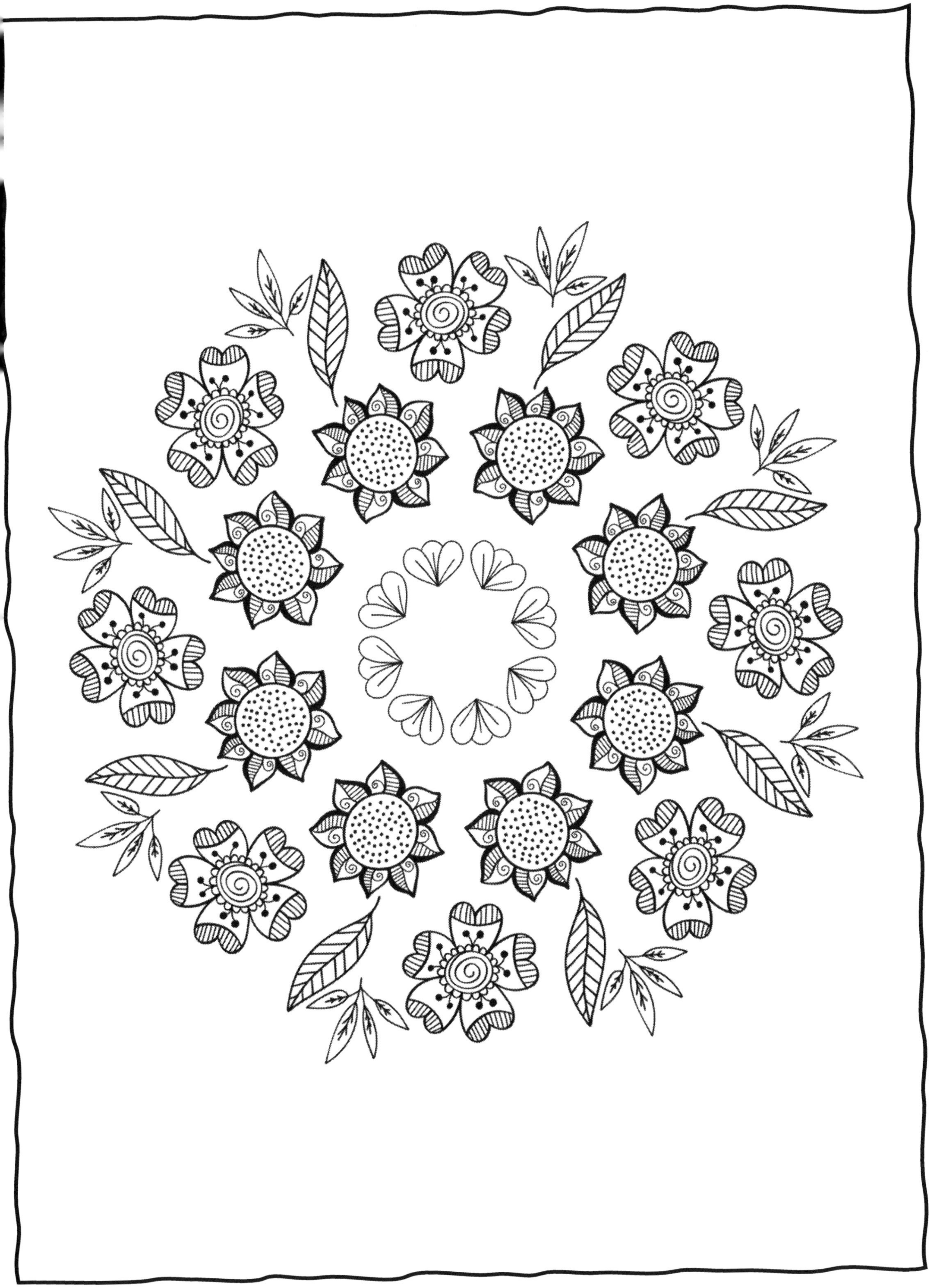

Don't Stop

TILL YOU GET THERE!

take easy

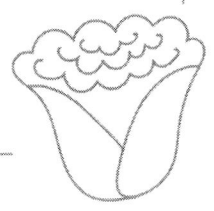

What are the top 5 places you want to visit?

1.

2.

3.

4.

5.

you are
OUT
of this
WORLD

Treat Yourself

Beautiful!

Appreciate | Attract | Achieve
Share Below
3 things you are grateful for today
1 thing you want to attract today
1 thing you want to achieve today!

3 things I'm grateful for today:

1.
2.
3.

1 thing I would love to attract into my day today:

1 thing I want to achieve today:

love

Follow

THE SUCCESS CLUES!

Let's Go

What's 2 things you achieved today that you're proud of?

1.

2.

breathe

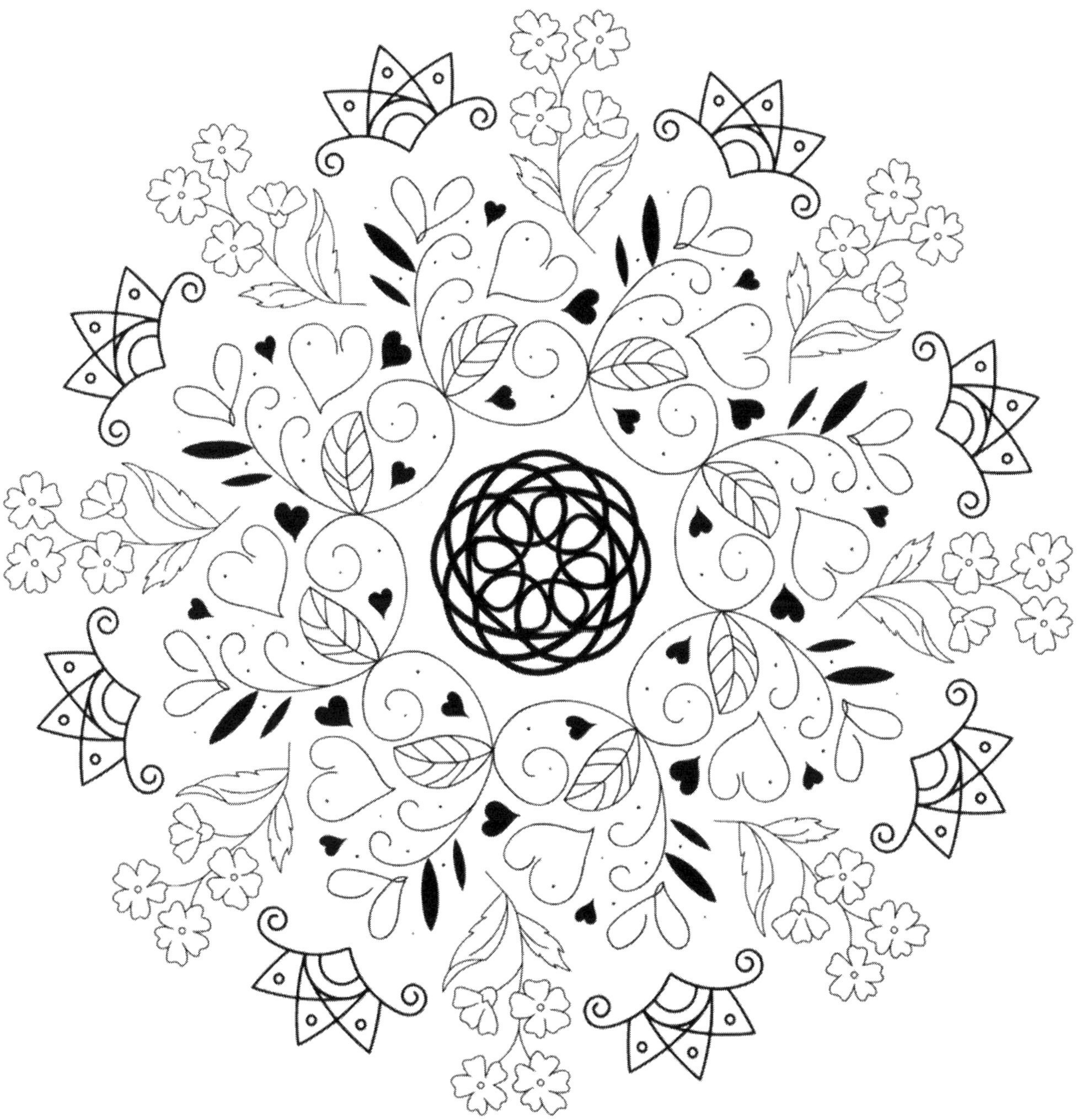

Empowered!

Appreciate | Attract | Achieve

Share Below

3 things you are grateful for today

1 thing you want to attract today

1 thing you want to achieve today!

3 things I'm grateful for today:

1.
2.
3.

1 thing I would love to attract into my day today:

1 thing I want to achieve today:

YOU
matter

NEVER give up

You're

ALMOST THERE
KEEP GOING!

start somewhere

3 things you are grateful for today...

DO YOUR THING

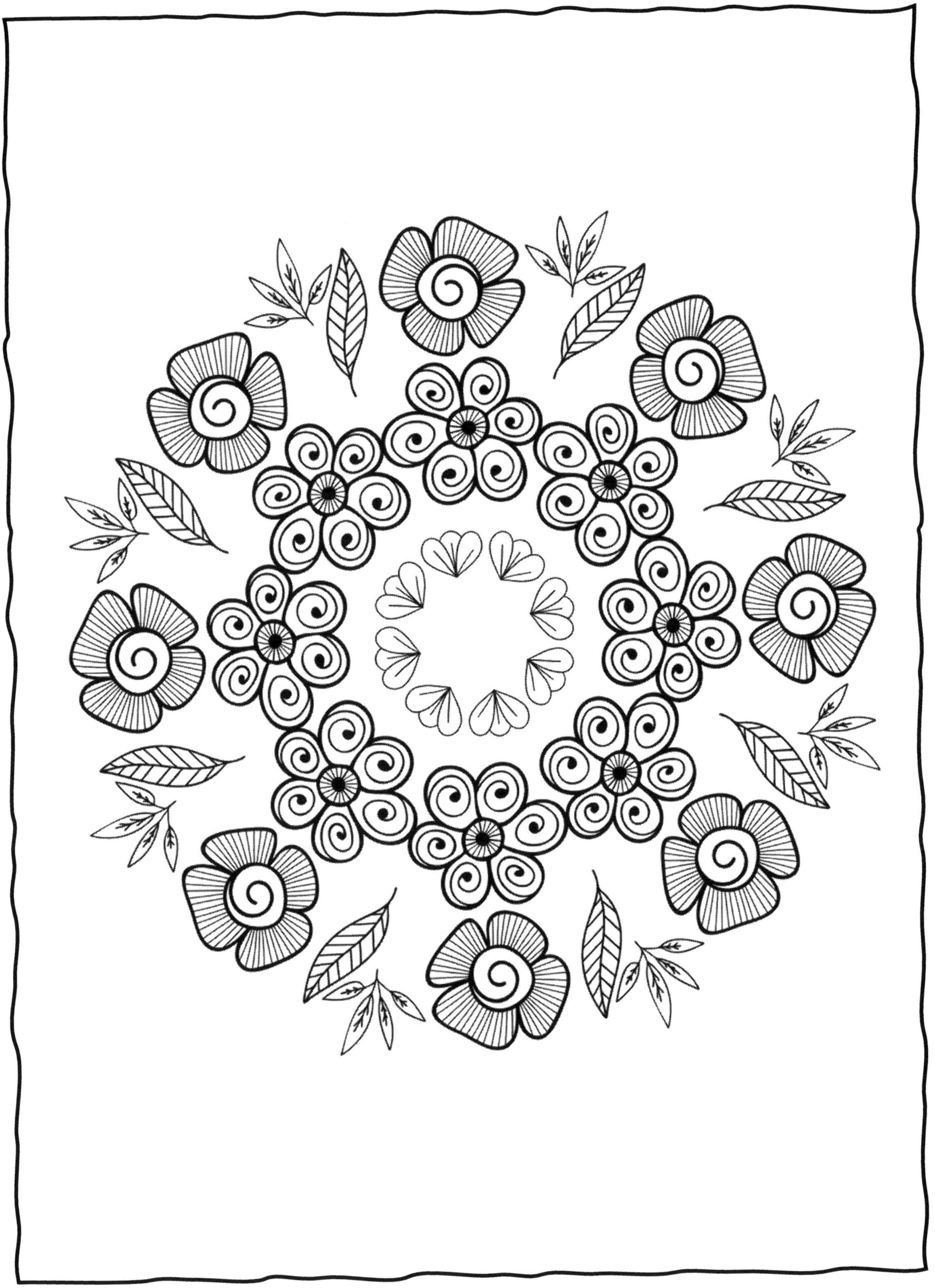

Evolving!

Appreciate | Attract | Achieve
Share Below
3 things you are grateful for today
1 thing you want to attract today
1 thing you want to achieve today!

3 things I'm grateful for today:

1.
2.
3.

1 thing I would love to attract into my day today:

1 thing I want to achieve today:

Rise and Shine

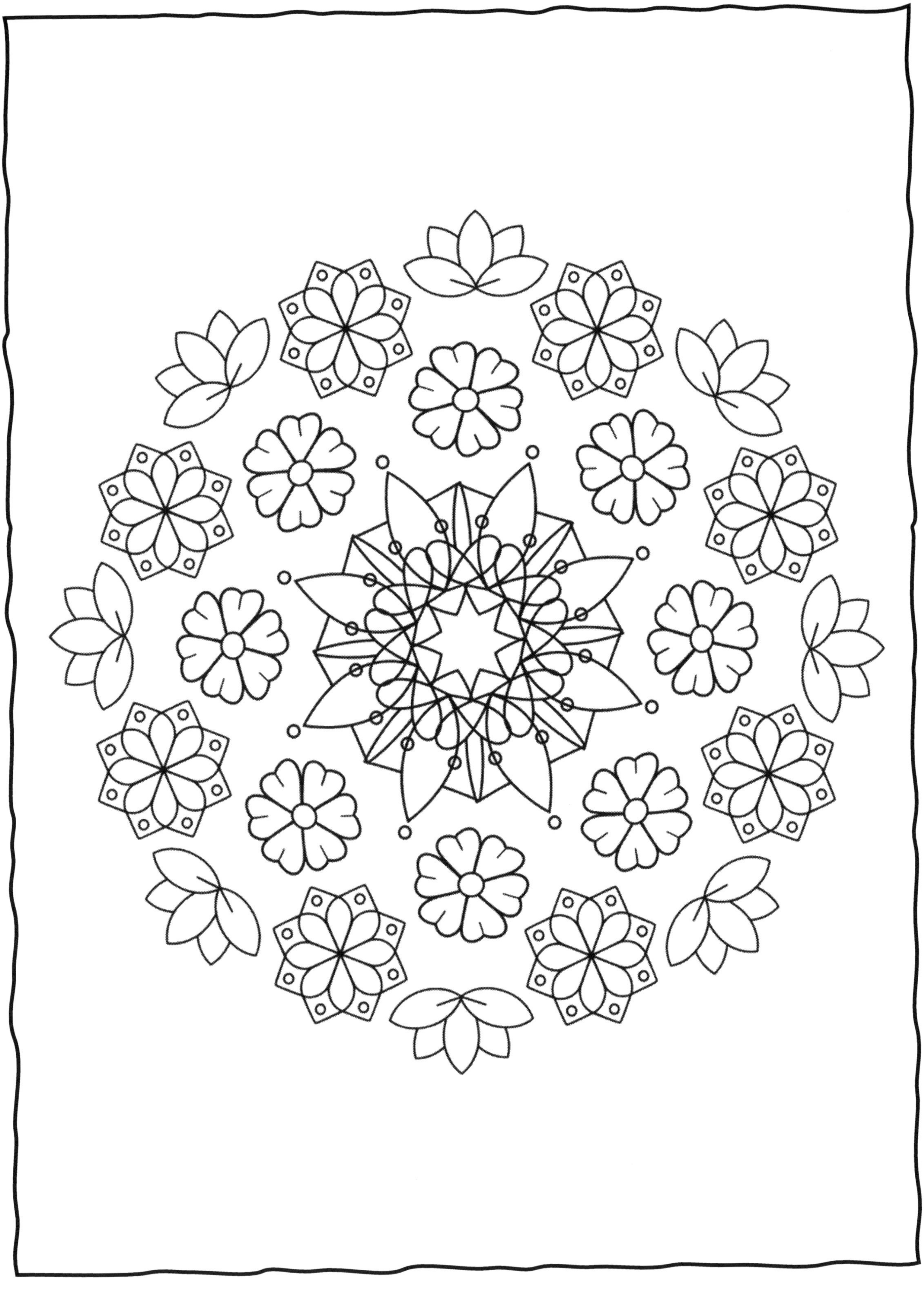

Believe

IT'S POSSIBLE, ALWAYS!

What is one big audacious goal you would love to achieve in the next 12 months and why is it important?

1.

Why?

Prove them wrong

YOU'RE
ink-credible

Brave!

Appreciate | Attract | Achieve

Share Below

3 things you are grateful for today

1 thing you want to attract today

1 thing you want to achieve today!

3 things I'm grateful for today:

1.
2.
3.

1 thing I would love to attract into my day today:

1 thing I want to achieve today:

IF NOT,
NOW
WHEN?

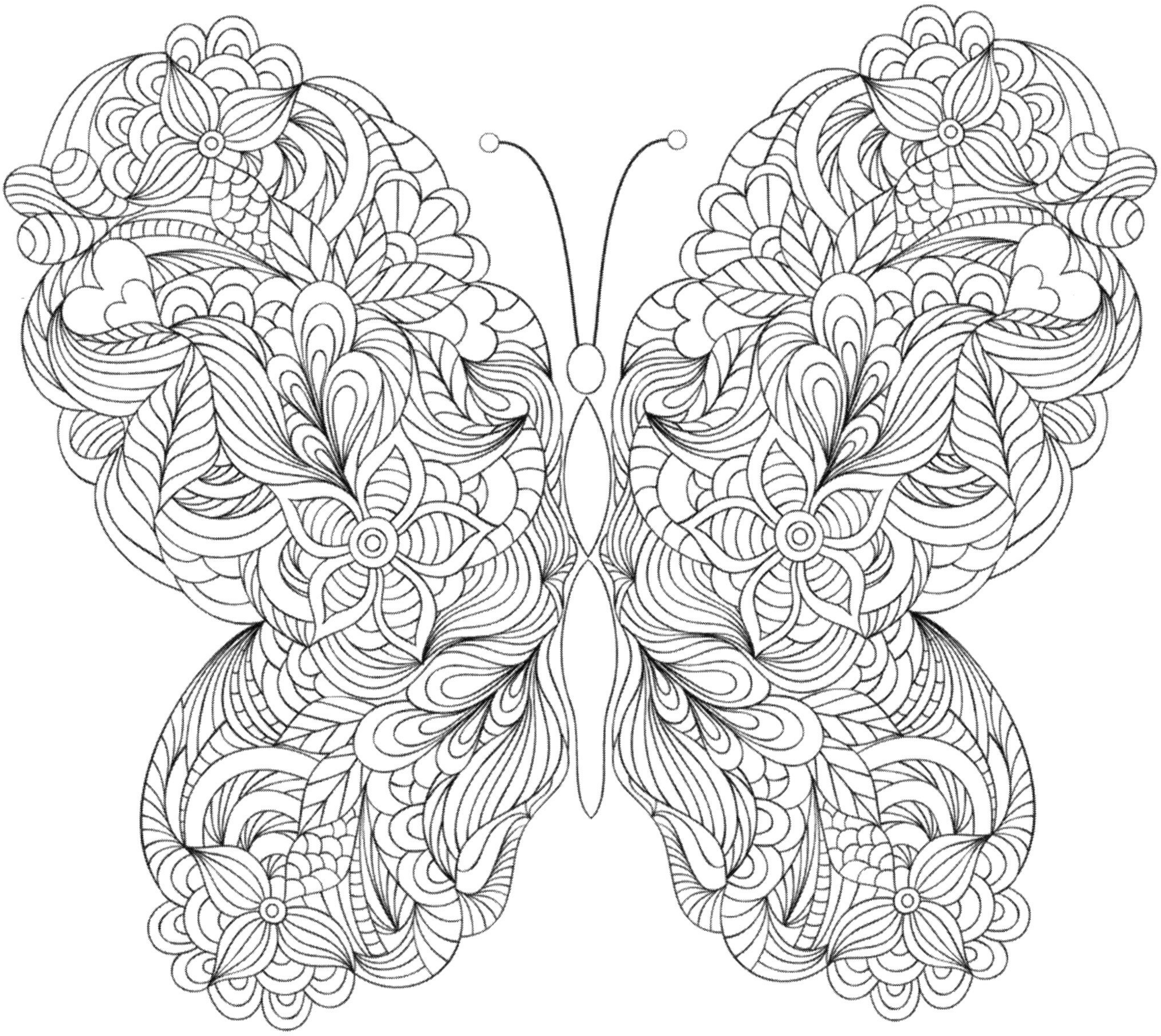

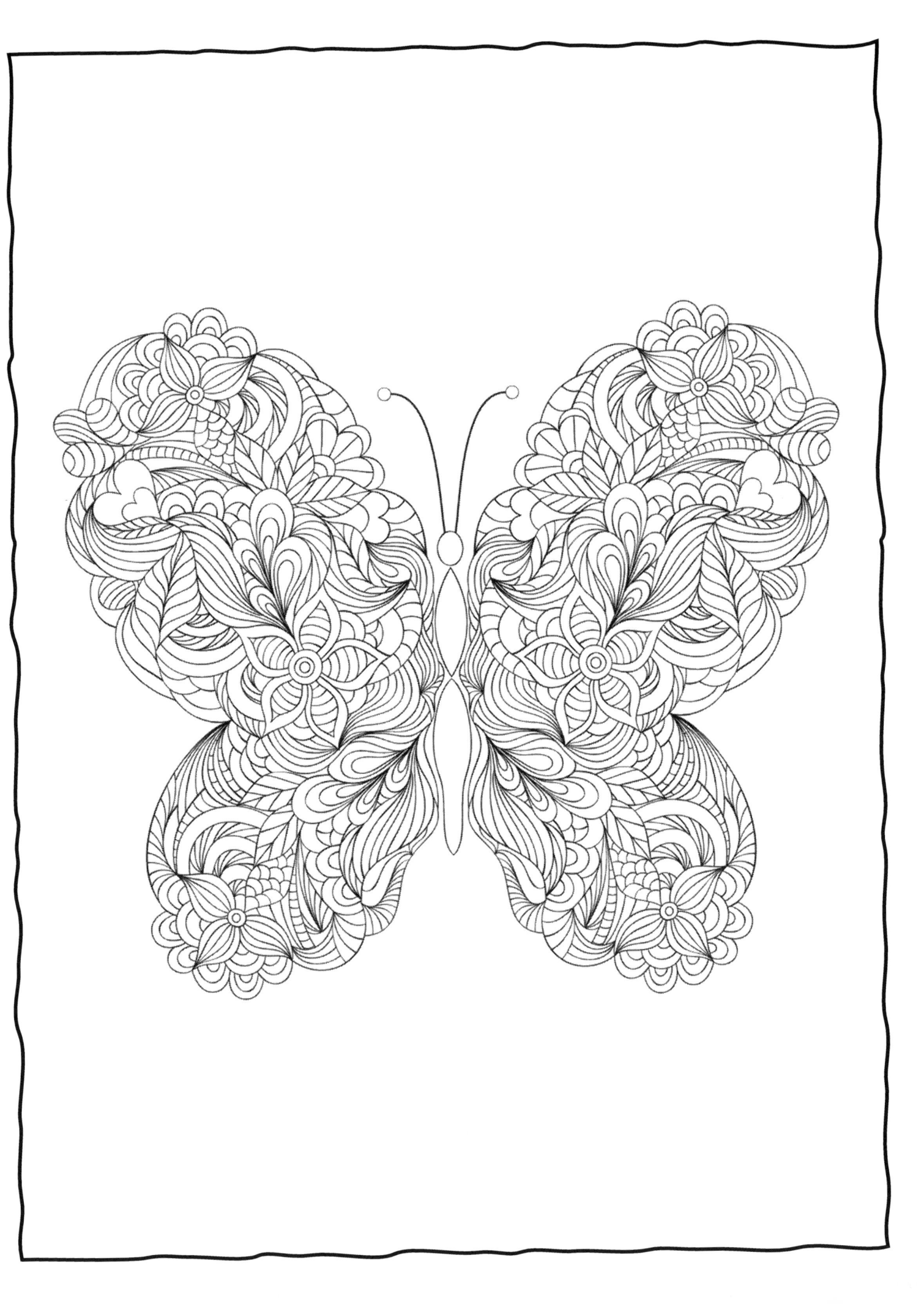

Listen

TO YOUR INNER VOICE!

Write down 3 of your favourite quotes

HAPPY THOUGHTS

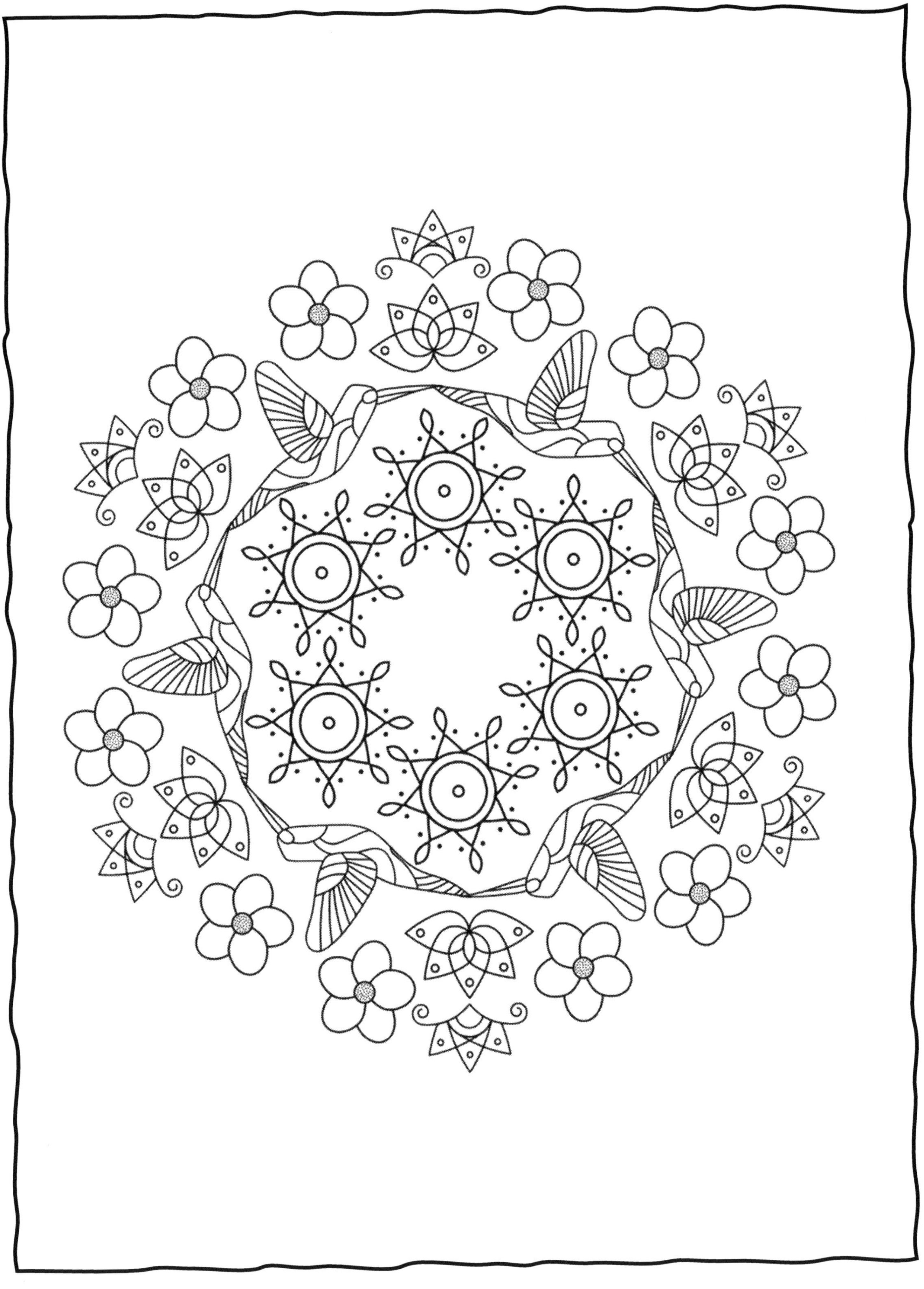

Passionate!

Appreciate | Attract | Achieve

Share Below

3 things you are grateful for today

1 thing you want to attract today

1 thing you want to achieve today!

3 things I'm grateful for today:

1.

2.

3.

1 thing I would love to attract into my day today:

1 thing I want to achieve today:

today is a New day

BE KIND

Your Heart

WILL GUIDE YOU!

Share one of the funniest things that ever happened to you and why it made you laugh

I BELeaf IN YOU!

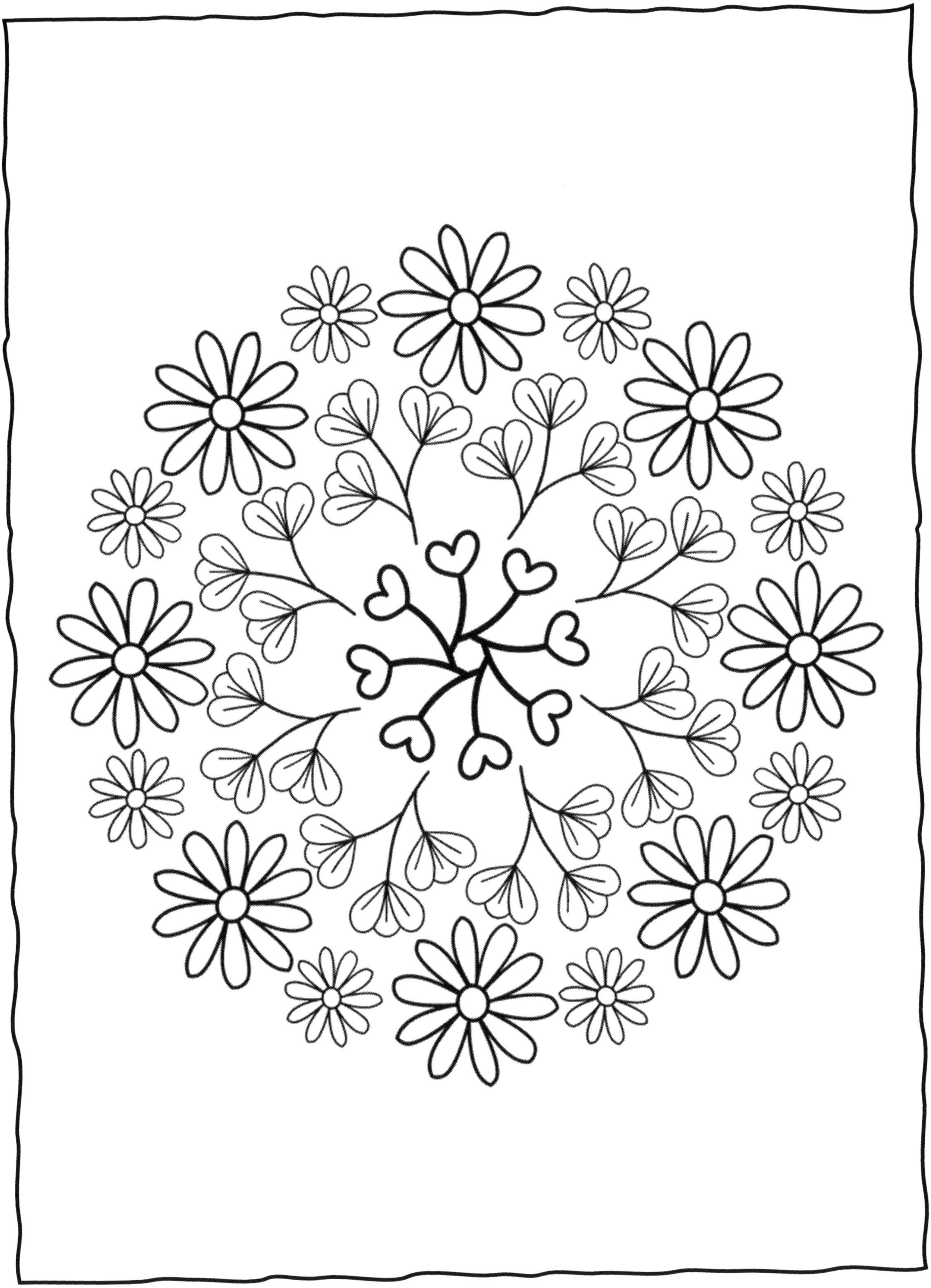

Star!

Appreciate | Attract | Achieve

Share Below

3 things you are grateful for today

1 thing you want to attract today

1 thing you want to achieve today!

3 things I'm grateful for today:

1.
2.
3.

1 thing I would love to attract into my day today:

1 thing I want to achieve today:

DONUT WORRY
BE HAPPY

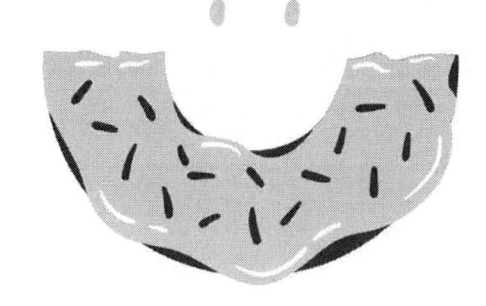

Follow the Stars.

Trust

THE JOURNEY YOU'RE ON

do what makes you happy

10 things that make you happy are?

1.
2.
3.
4.
5.
6.
7.
8.

YOU ARE
golden

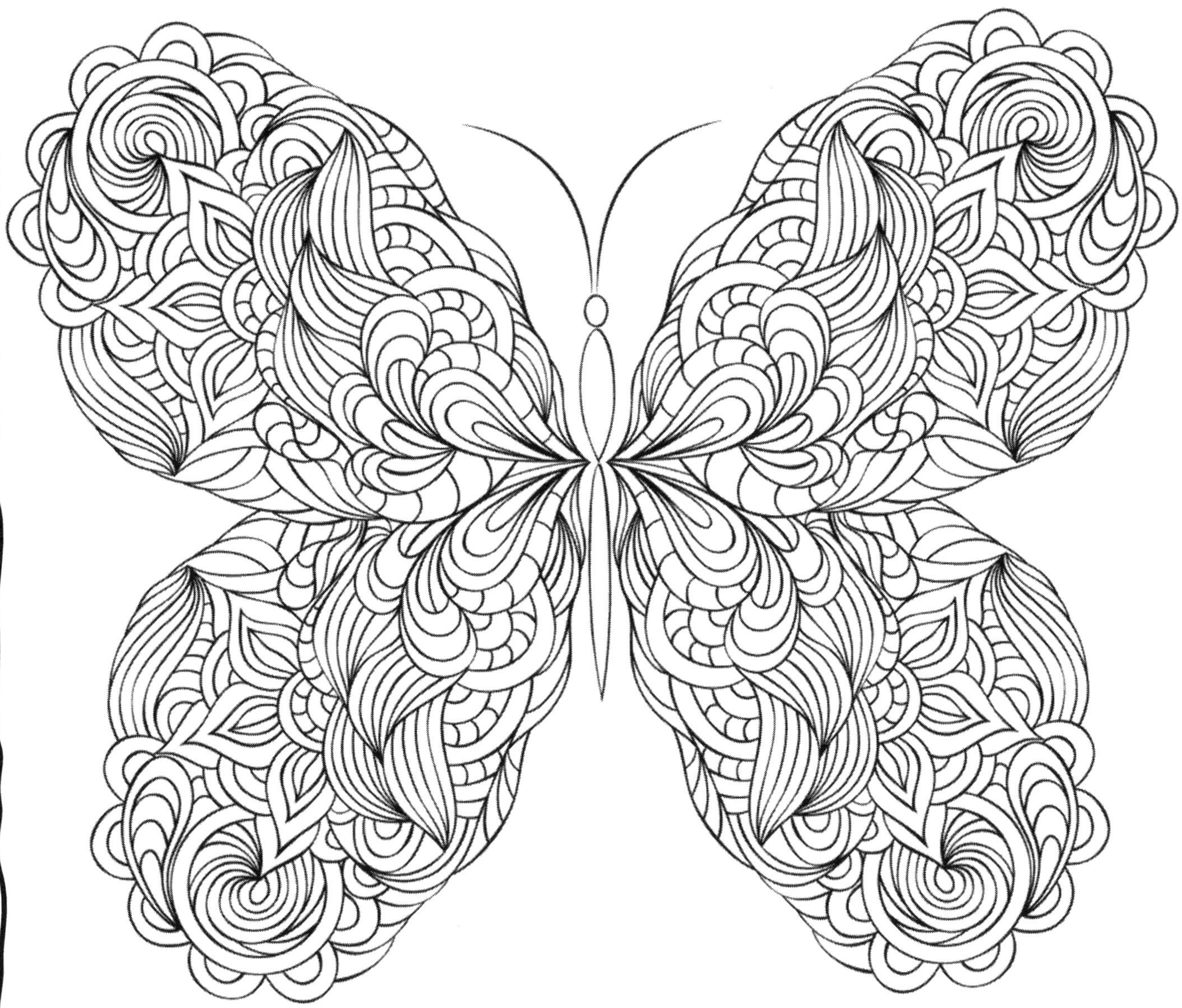

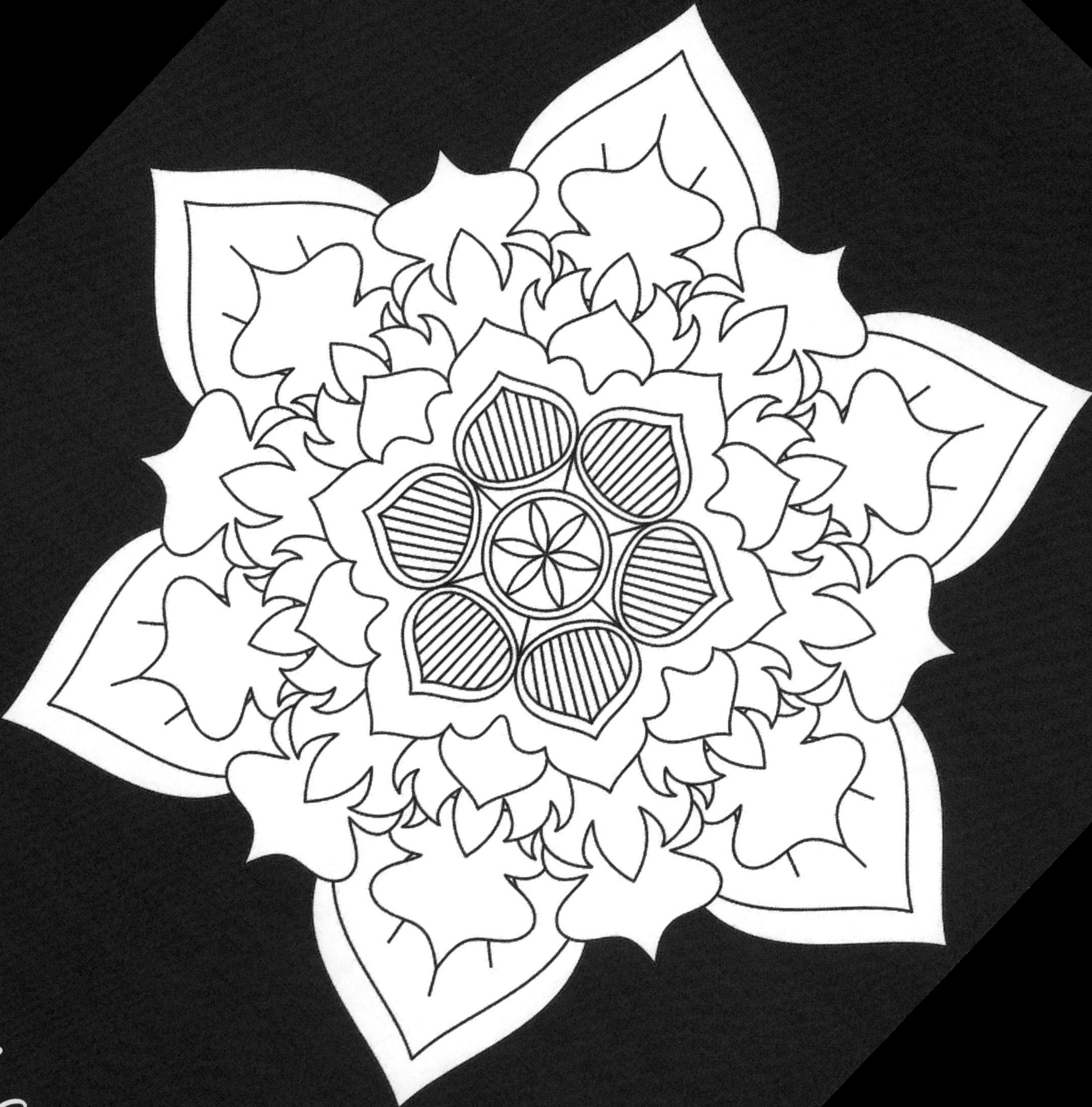

Appreciate | Attract | Achieve

Share Below

3 things you are grateful for today

1 thing you want to attract today

1 thing you want to achieve today!

3 things I'm grateful for today:

1.
2.
3.

1 thing I would love to attract into my day today:

1 thing I want to achieve today:

KNOW YOUR WORTH

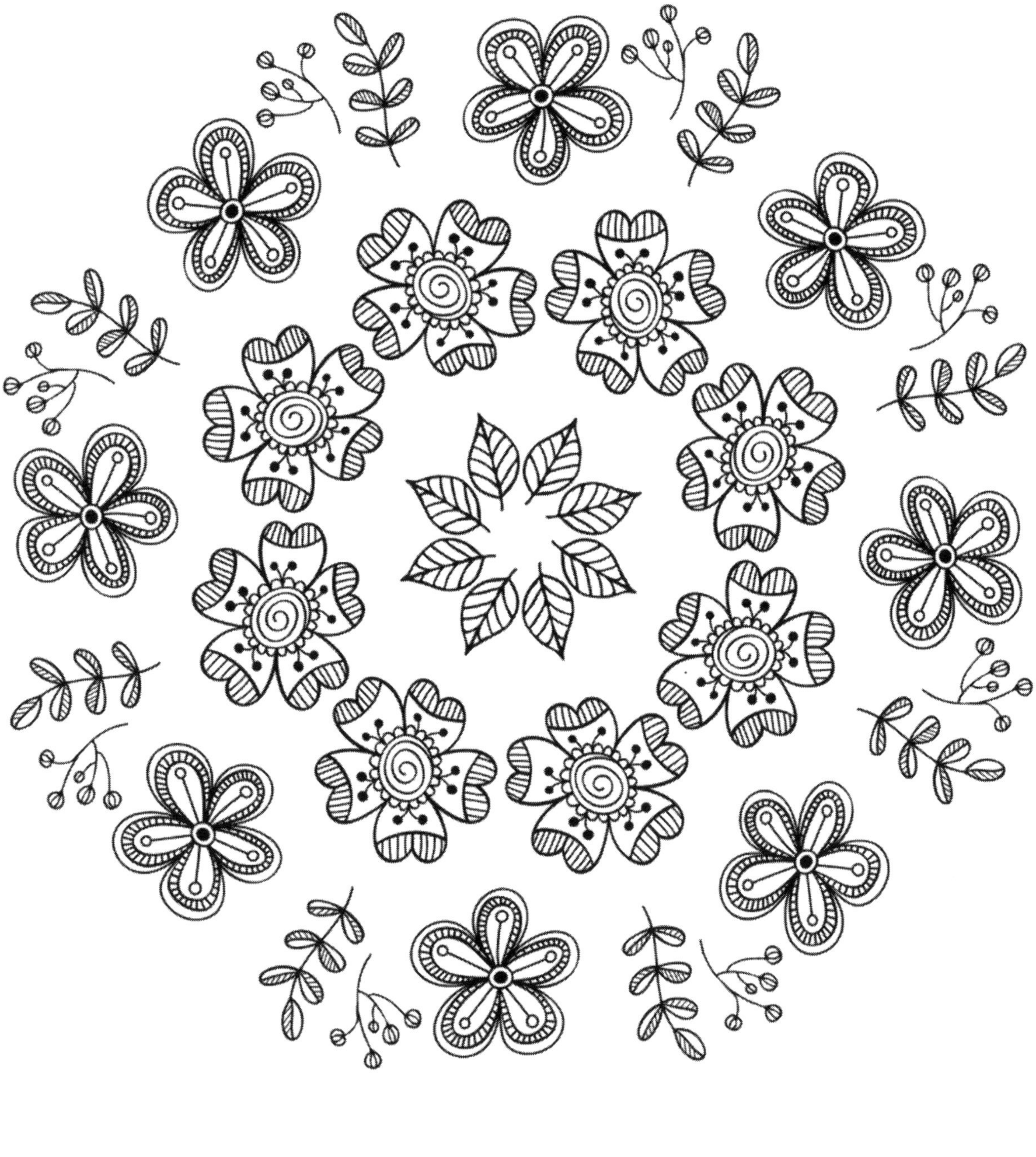

Happiness

COMES FROM YOU!

If you could describe your personality with only 4 inspirational words what would they be?

believe

Believe

Amazing!

Appreciate | Attract | Achieve

Share Below

3 things you are grateful for today

1 thing you want to attract today

1 thing you want to achieve today!

3 things I'm grateful for today:

1.
2.
3.

1 thing I would love to attract into my day today:

1 thing I want to achieve today:

DO
YOUR BEST

Best DAY ever!

Yes You Can!

OFF YOU GO

List your 5 favorite naughty foods and why you love it so much:

Love

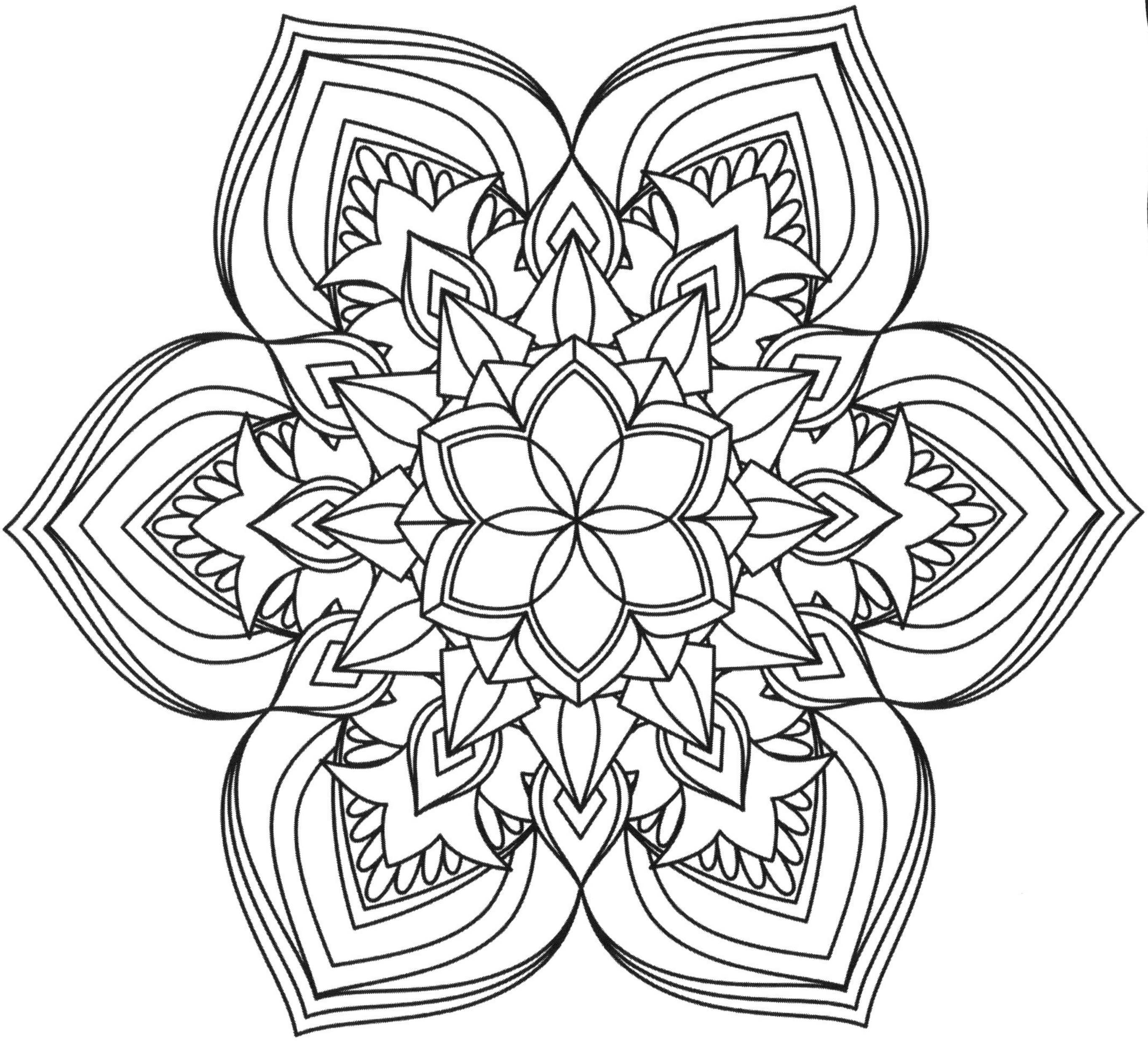

Magnificent!

Appreciate | Attract | Achieve

Share Below

3 things you are grateful for today

1 thing you want to attract today

1 thing you want to achieve today!

3 things I'm grateful for today:

1.
2.
3.

1 thing I would love to attract into my day today:

1 thing I want to achieve today:

i need Vitamin Sea

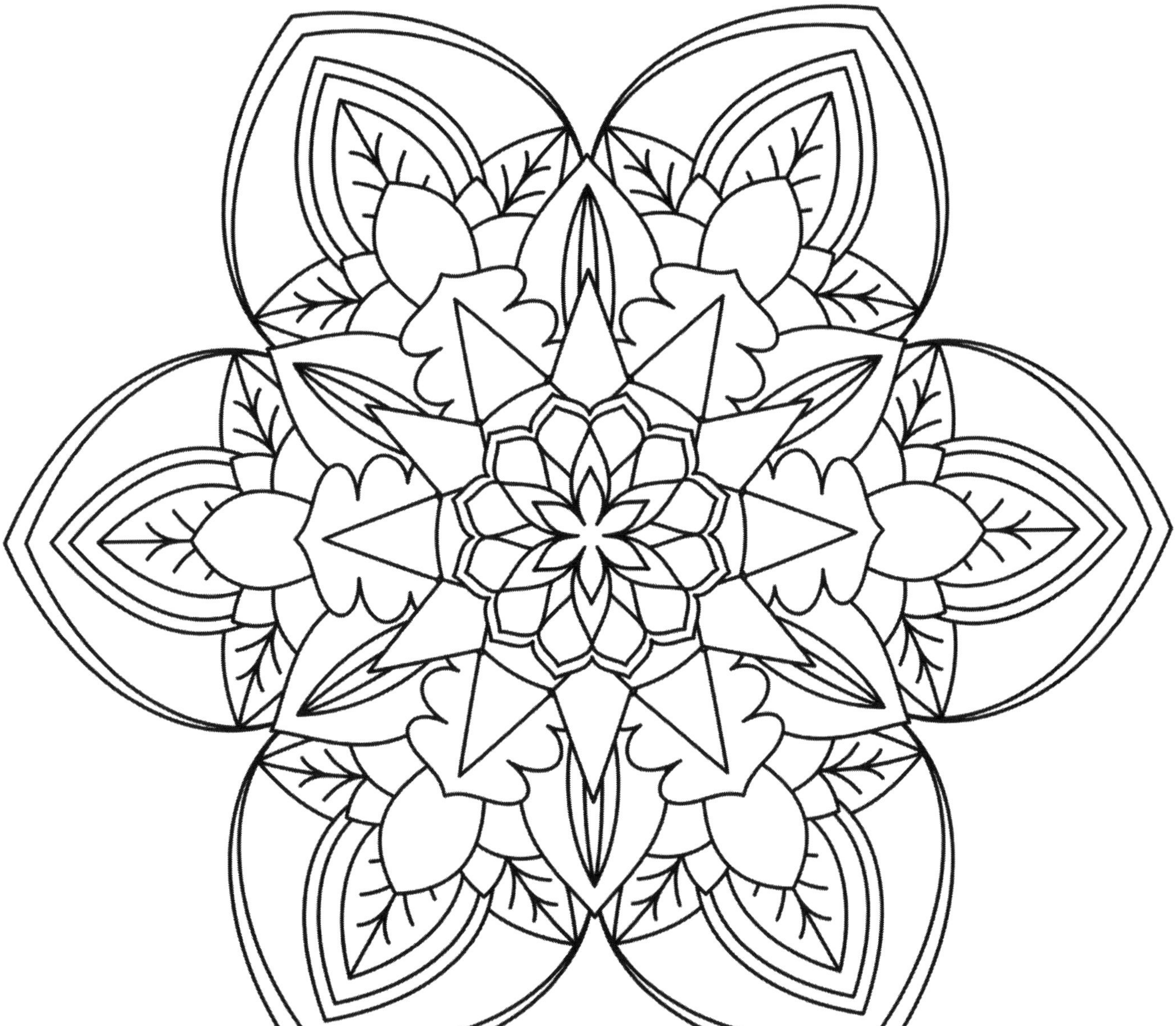

Live Your Life

EVERY DAY, SMILING!

Share a life changing moment in your life and why it helped you become who you are today:

Joy

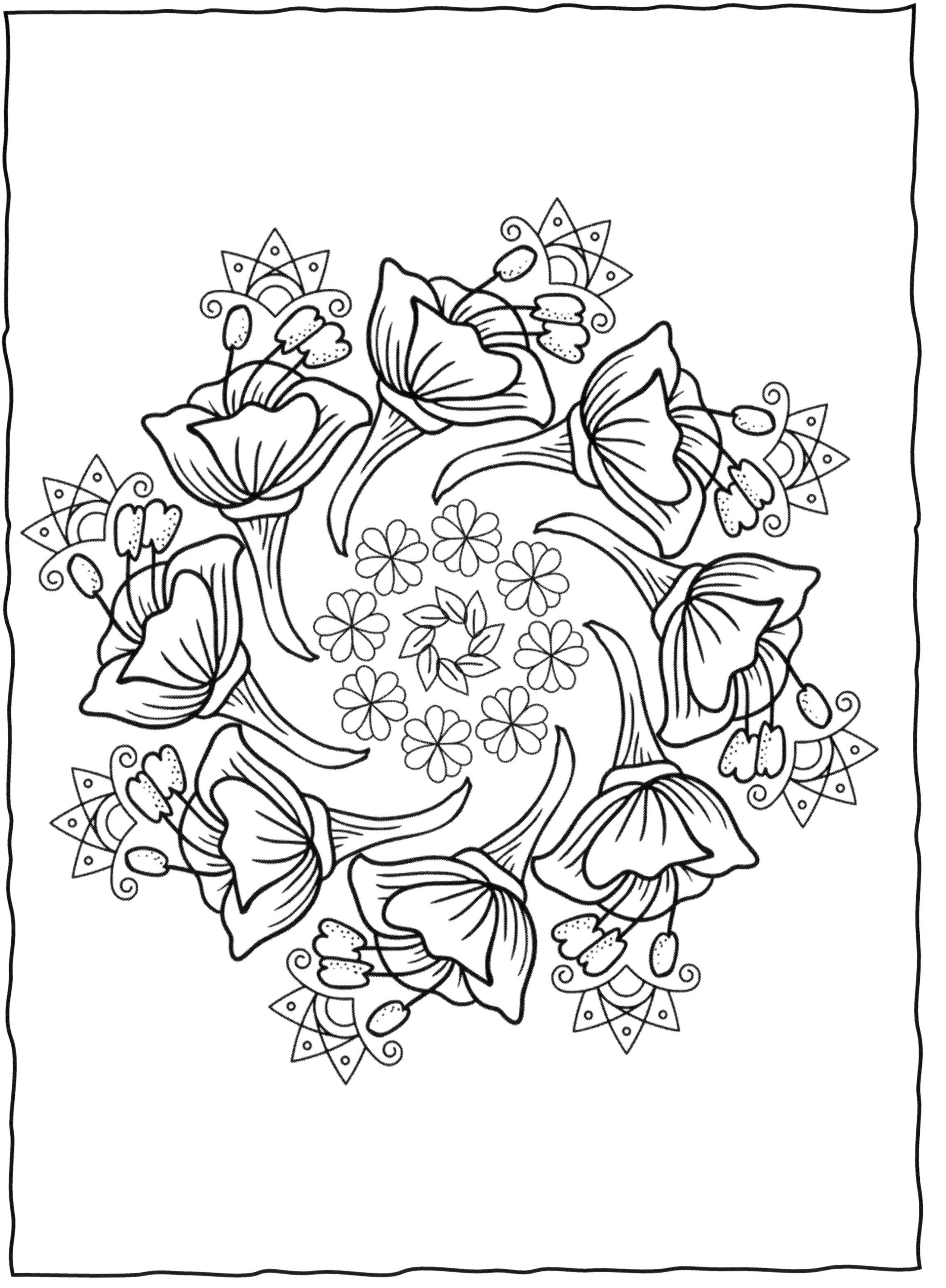

Selfless!

Appreciate | Attract | Achieve

Share Below

3 things you are grateful for today

1 thing you want to attract today

1 thing you want to achieve today!

3 things I'm grateful for today:

1.
2.
3.

1 thing I would love to attract into my day today:

1 thing I want to achieve today:

I WANNA BE A Unicorn

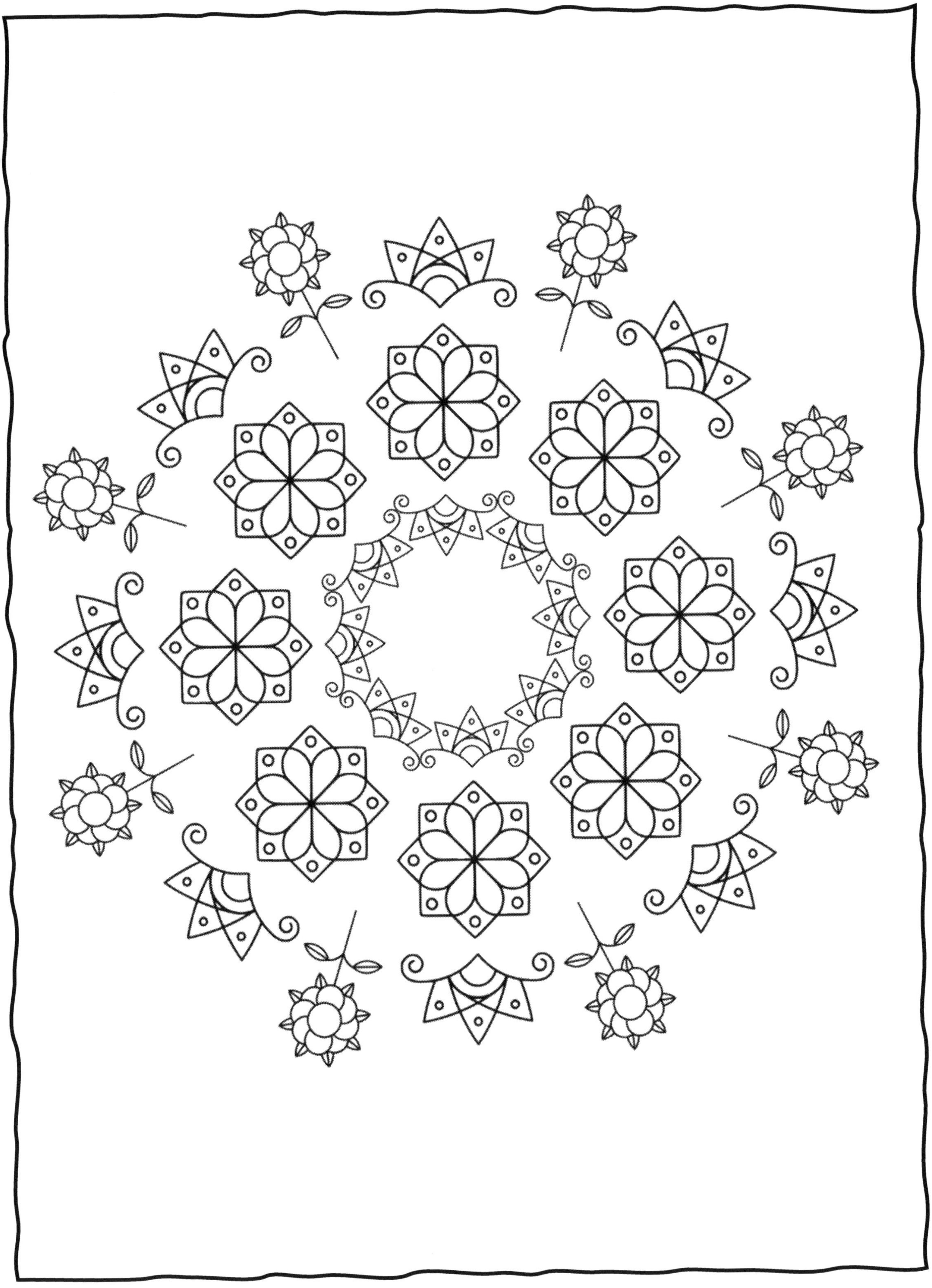

Good morning

BEAUTIFUL

You just won a million dollars what is the first 5 things you would spend it on?

1.

2.

3.

4.

5.

Mermaid at Heart

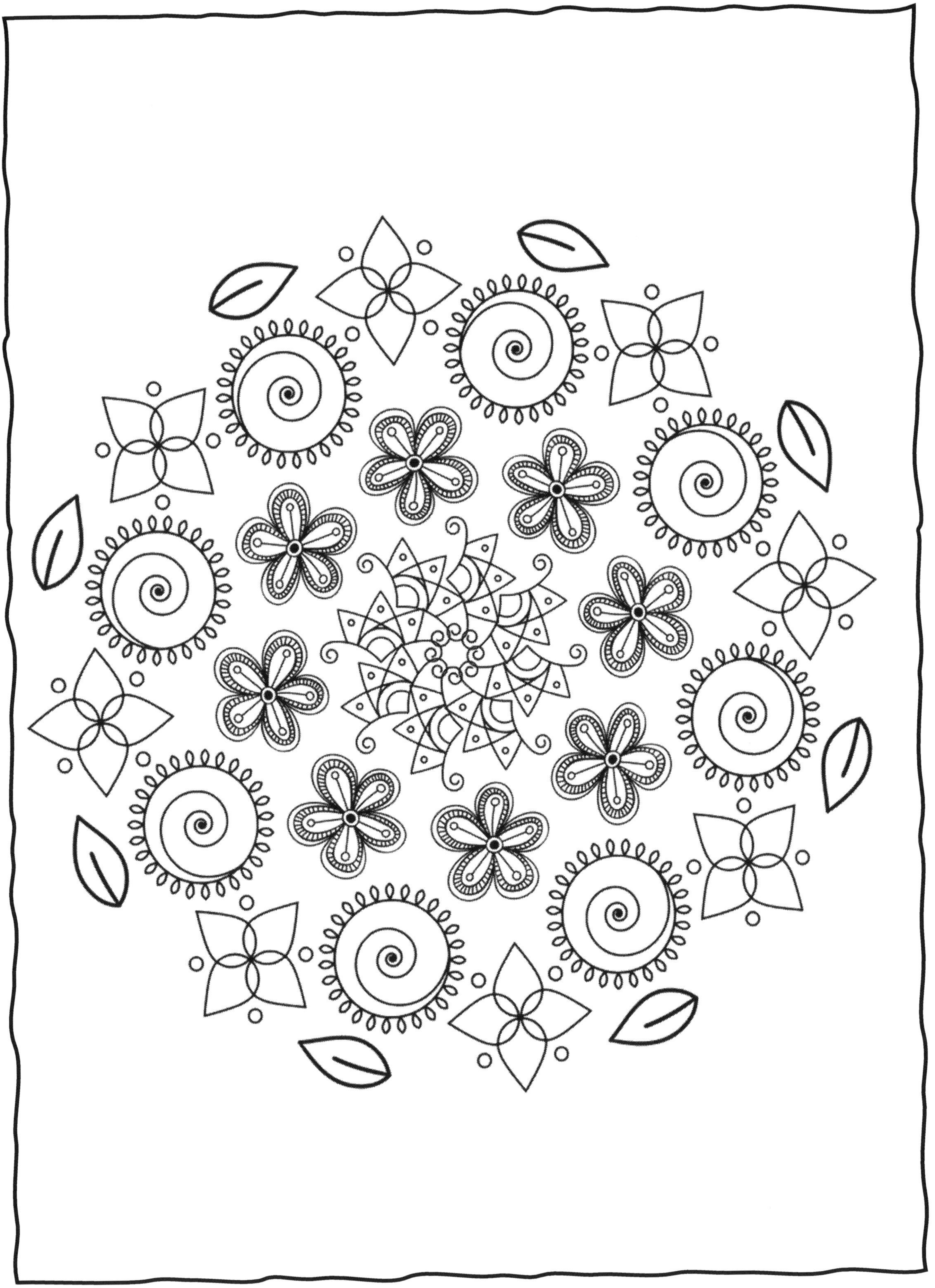

Extraordinary!

Appreciate | Attract | Achieve

Share Below

3 things you are grateful for today

1 thing you want to attract today

1 thing you want to achieve today!

3 things I'm grateful for today:

1.
2.
3.

1 thing I would love to attract into my day today:

1 thing I want to achieve today:

grateful

MAKE today GREAT

Your Smile

IS MAGICAL!

What's your 3mth/ 6mth/ 12month money goals?

One Month: $

Six Month: $

Twelve Month: $

Be Brave

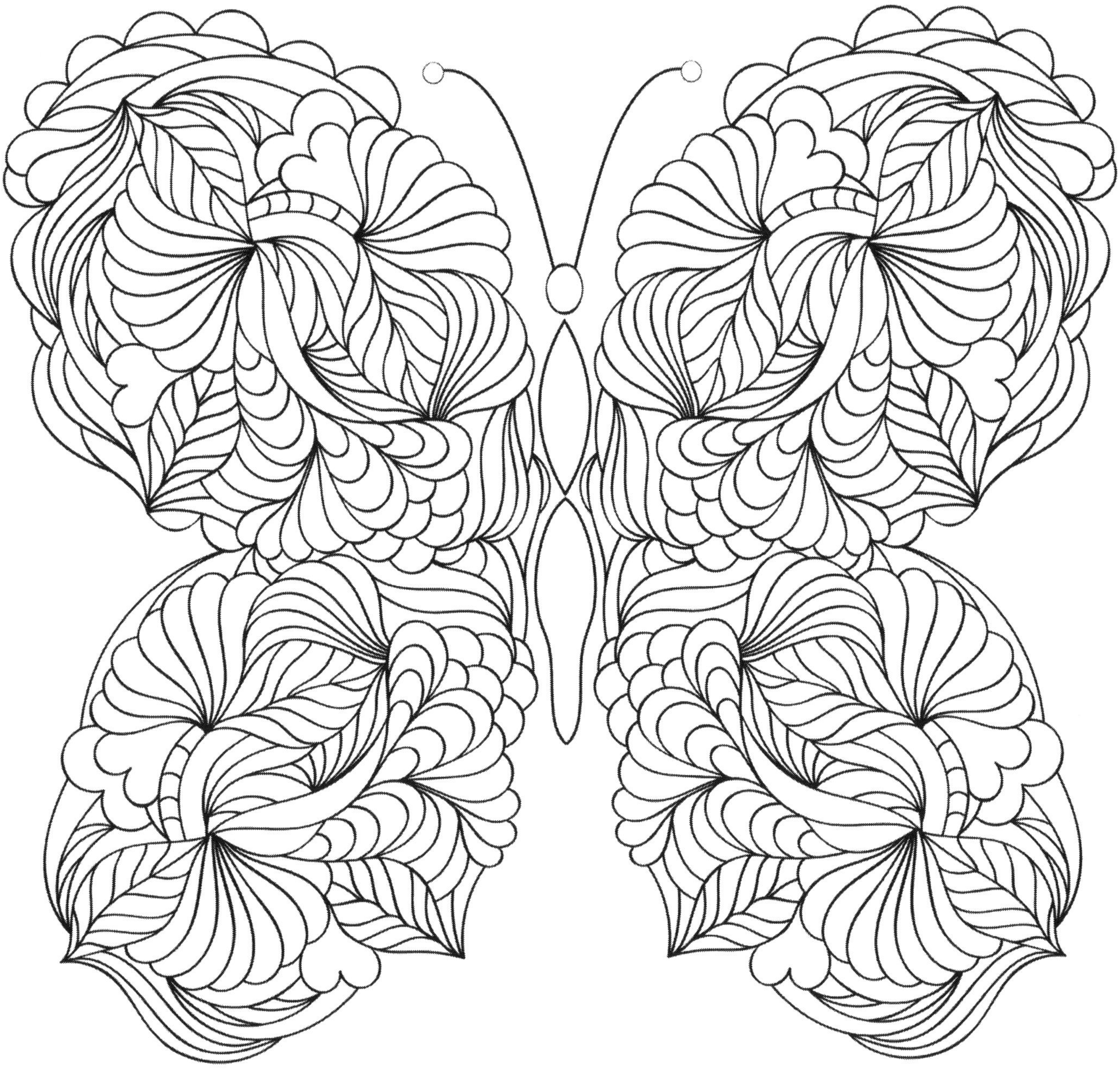

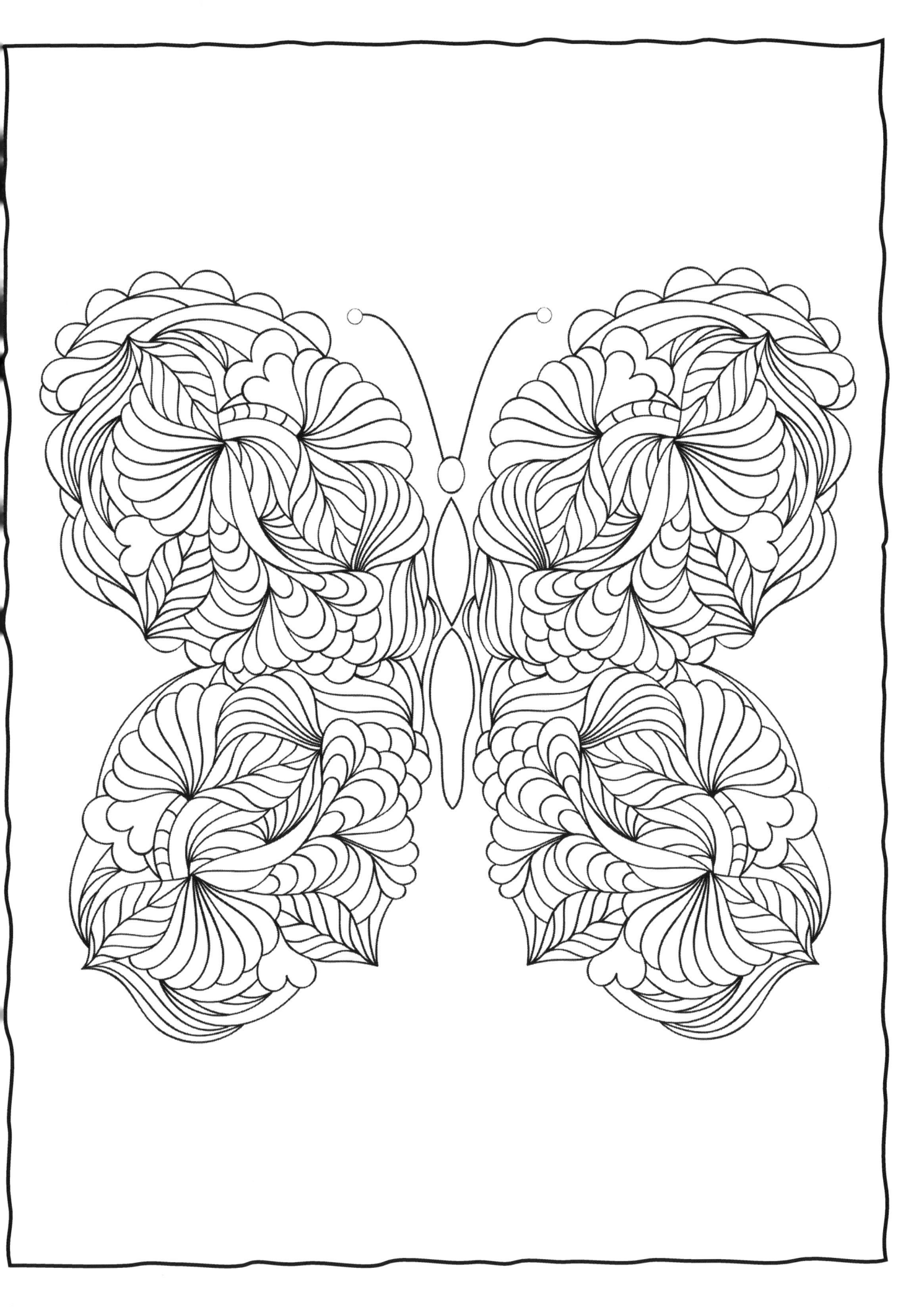

Smart!

Appreciate | Attract | Achieve

Share Below

3 things you are grateful for today

1 thing you want to attract today

1 thing you want to achieve today!

3 things I'm grateful for today:

1.
2.
3.

1 thing I would love to attract into my day today:

1 thing I want to achieve today:

DO Amazing THINGS!

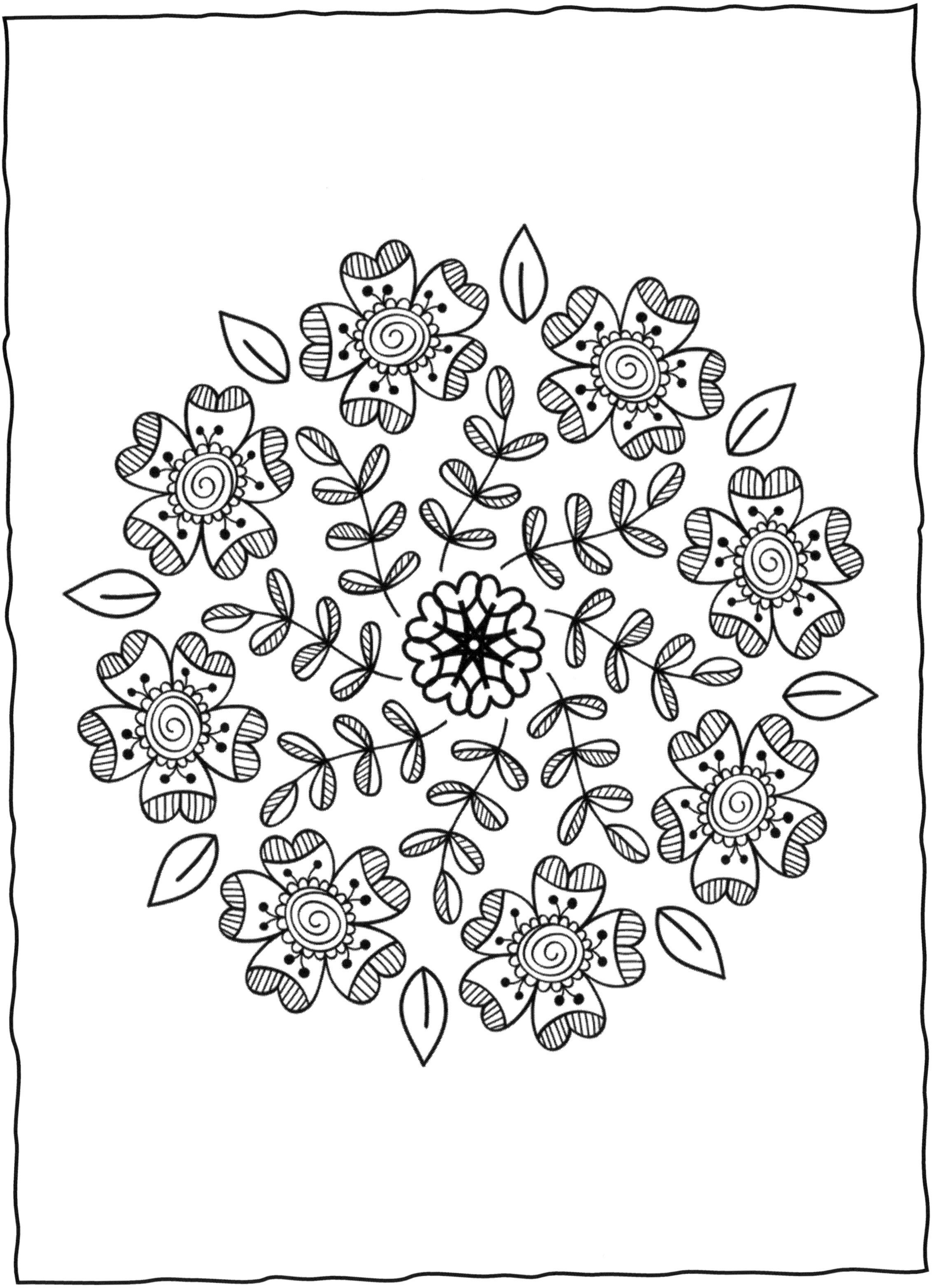

You're

AWESOME!

If you could relive one day in your life what would it be and why?

Wild Child

Let our lives be full of both thanks and giving

Gifted!

Appreciate | Attract | Achieve

Share Below

3 things you are grateful for today

1 thing you want to attract today

1 thing you want to achieve today!

3 things I'm grateful for today:

1.
2.
3.

1 thing I would love to attract into my day today:

1 thing I want to achieve today:

MAKE IT HAPPEN

no bad days

You're

IMPERFECTLY PERFECT
YAY!

Please make sure to visit:

https://pambrossman.com/pbjournals

To see the other notebooks, journals, planners and adult coloring books in the **Evolving HQ series.**

COPYRIGHT © PAMBROSSMAN.COM - ALL RIGHTS RESERVED WORLDWIDE.
THIS PRODUCT IS PROTECTED UNDER INTERNATIONAL AND NATIONAL
COPYRIGHT LAWS 2020

Made in the USA
Columbia, SC
10 December 2023